PARENTING FOREVER WORKBOOK

Materials were adapted from A Parenting Guidebook

BY

DR. WILLIE J. GREER KIMMONS
DR. GAYLE S. INGRAHAM

authorHOUSE

AuthorHouse™
1663 Liberty Drive
Bloomington, IN 47403
www.authorhouse.com
Phone: 833-262-8899

Published by AuthorHouse 03/11/2022

ISBN: 978-1-6655-3556-4 (sc)
ISBN: 978-1-6655-3555-7 (e)

A TRAINING WORKBOOK
FOR PARENTS, GRANDPARENTS, TEACHERS, SCHOOLS, CHURCHES,
COMMUNITY GROUPS, DAY CARE CENTERS, HEAD START PROGRAMS
AND CIVIC GROUPS

**A WORKBOOK WITH STEP BY STEP
PROCESSES FOR PROVIDING GUIDELINES TO BUILDING AND
DEVELOPING PRODUCTIVE AND SUCCESSFUL CHILDREN**

CONTENTS

DEDICATION

This Parenting Forever Workbook Training Program is dedicated to all the parents, grandparents and significant adults in the home. It is important to address our children problems while they are young and to assist them as they become older youth in society to become successful and crime free. The training program for parents will be 3 Saturdays, 8am-5pm, to provide useful strategies, suggestions and recommendations for them to learn how to be better parents for their children. There will be 7 well detailed training modules for parents to participate in during the 3 Saturdays. It doesn't matter if the parent is rich or poor, young or old, married or single or formally educated or not, parents, grandparents or significant adults in the household is the most important person to that child. This is why this Parenting Forever Workbook is dedicated to parents and all concerned citizens and community leaders who are interested in the growth and development of children.

Dr. Willie J. Greer Kimmons and Dr. Gayle S. Ingraham

ABOUT THE AUTHORS

DR. WILLIE J. GREER KIMMONS
Biography

Speaker

Author

Educator

Administrator

Military Officer

Parent/Grandparent

Health Spokesperson

Community Activist

Humanitarian

"A STRONG VOICE FOR OUR CHILDREN, PARENTS AND TEACHERS"

Dr. Willie J. Kimmons was born in Hernando, Mississippi. He was raised in Memphis, Tennessee where he attended public schools and received his high school diploma from Frederick Douglass High School. He was a student athlete and received an athletic scholarship to attend Lincoln University in Jefferson City, Missouri. While at Lincoln University, he was active in the Student Government Association and ROTC. He served as First Lieutenant in the United States Army, Adjutant General Corps, during the Vietnam era as an administrative, data processing, and personnel officer.

Dr. Kimmons received his undergraduate education at Lincoln University in Jefferson City, Missouri, in Health Education and Psychology. He received his Master's Degree in Curriculum and Instruction and his Doctorate Degree in Educational Administration and Supervision in Higher Education at the age of 28 from Northern Illinois University in DeKalb, Illinois.

Dr. Kimmons has served at every level in the higher education teaching and learning process with dedication and distinction. Over the past forty years, he has been a Classroom Teacher; superintendent of schools; a College Professor; College President and College Chancellor.

Currently he is serving as an Educational Consultant for Pre-K-16 schools, author and as a Motivational/Empowerment speaker. Dr. Kimmons also serves as consultant in the areas of Title I programs; parental involvement; teacher and administrative training. He provides consultant services for public and private schools, two and four-year colleges and universities throughout the country. He is one of America's leading authorities on education, leadership, parental involvement, and health related issues. He is a nationally recognized consultant, speaker, seminar leader, and author of seven (7) books.

Dr. Kimmons made his <u>first</u> of many presentations at the National Alliance of Black School Educators Conference in Miami, Florida in <u>1974.</u> He has given more than 500 presentations and lectures to a variety of organizations including: educational associations; Chambers of Commerce; elementary, middle, and high schools; 2 year colleges, 4 year colleges, and universities; churches and other religious organizations; Kiwanis; Rotary; Lions; NAACP; Urban League; economic development organizations; political groups; Greek organizations; youth groups; parenting groups; daycare centers; Head Start programs; civic and other community organizations.

Dr. Kimmons serves as a health care advocate. He is a national spokesperson and proposal reviewer for diabetes, breast and prostate cancers, and health related matters and he serves on the African American Men's Health Summit, Steering Committee for Central Florida. He is a member of the Volusia and Flagler Counties African American Men's Prostate Cancer Board of Directors, Daytona Beach, Florida.

Dr. Kimmons is Vice-Chairperson of the Daytona Beach Community Relations Council; Vice-Chairperson of Daytona Beach/Volusia County Association for Retarded Citizens; Board member of Daytona Beach/ Volusia County Health Department; Vice President of the Volusia County Florida Men Against Destruction-Defending Against Drugs and

Social Disorder, (MAD DADS); Facilitator of "Young Male's Rites of Passage Program", Greater Friendship Baptist Church, Daytona Beach, Florida; Board member of the Daytona Beach/Volusia County Salvation Army; Vice President, Volusia County Florida First Step Juvenile Residential Facility for young males; Board member of Volusia County Florida Children and Family Services; Committee member, Orlando, Orange County Florida, Juvenile Delinquency, Truancy, Crime and Behavioral Issues in Schools; and Committee member, Orlando, Orange County Florida, Juvenile Commission for Mental Health and Substance Abuse in Schools; Chair of the Board, Daytona Beach Housing Authority; Co-Chair, Daytona Beach, FL Charter Review Commission. Policy Council Board Member of Mid-Florida Community Services, Inc. Head Start, DeLand, Florida.

Dr. Kimmons was selected in 2001 as a Distinguished Alumnus of his Alma Mater, Lincoln University, a Historical Black Institution located in Jefferson City, Missouri. He was recognized for his leadership skills, community involvement, scholarly pursuits, and educational achievements as an author, college professor, motivational speaker, college president and chancellor. In addition, the Distinguished Graduate award was bestowed upon Dr. Kimmons for exemplary service and for his contributions as an outstanding alumnus. The National Association for Equal Opportunity in Higher Education (NAFEO), also honored Dr. Kimmons at its 26th National Conference on Blacks in Higher Education held in Washington, D. C. in March, 2001.

Dr. Kimmons was the 2003 recipient of the <u>Furthering Rights, Investing in Equality and Nurturing Diversity</u> (F.R.I.E.N.D.) Award in Orlando Florida. The Florida Civil Rights and Human Relations Commission honored him for his outstanding mentoring and volunteer work in public schools and the community.

Dr. Kimmons was the 2006 recipient of the National Alliance of Black School Educators, (NABSE), and Lifetime Achievement Award. NABSE honored him for his outstanding lifetime efforts and achievements to the African American community and the community at-large. This award was bestowed upon Dr. Kimmons at NABSE's Annual National Conference in Orlando, Florida.

Dr. Kimmons was inducted in the Frederick Douglass High School 2008 Wall of Fame for his scholarly pursuits, leadership skills, educational attainments in public schools, 2 and 4-year colleges and universities and as an honored graduate in Memphis, Tennessee.

Dr. Kimmons was honored as an outstanding community leader by the Daytona Deliverance Church of God in Daytona Beach, Florida, August, 2010. He was honored for his lifetime commitment of working with young people in the Volusia County Florida school system as a mentor and volunteer and his leadership in community activities, serving on numerous boards and advisory councils. He was commended for his service as a humanitarian, health care advocate and community activist which enriched the city, county and state in which he resides.

Dr. Kimmons was honored as a distinguished graduate by Northern Illinois University College of Education in DeKalb, IL in September, 2011.

Dr. Willie Kimmons was recognized in 2012 by the National Alumni Association of Frederick Douglass High School for his continuous outstanding commitment and dedication to Frederick Douglass High School in Memphis, TN.

In 2013, Dr. Kimmons served as honored guest speaker on the Central Florida Good Life Television Program, channel 45, viewed by more than 5 million viewers in Orlando, FL.

Dr. Kimmons was honored as the Father of the Year at the 16th Annual International Fatherhood Conference and served as keynote speaker in June 2014 in Memphis, TN.

Dr. Kimmons was honored in 2016 as a former president of Trenholm State Community College in Montgomery, Alabama at the 50th Anniversary Celebration of the College. (1966-2016) for his professional commitment and dedication in stabilizing the College under his leadership as President.

2017, Dr. Kimmons published his 6th book, "The Making of an Urban Community College in a Union and Political Environment: A Historical Perspective of Wayne County Community District, Detroit, Michigan (1964-2017), where he served as President (1979-1983).

2018, Dr. Kimmons was the recipient of the National Civil Rights and Social Justice Award for his lifelong commitment and his body of work in support of human dignity, civil rights and social justice. The award was presented during the 54th Anniversary Commemorative Service for James Chaney, Andrew Goodman and Michael Schwerner, the three young freedom fighters who were lynched in 1964 in Philadelphia, Mississippi. Dr. Kimmons also served as the keynote speaker at the awards ceremony.

2020, Dr. Kimmons served on the Daytona Beach, Florida Branch of the NAACP, Board and Executive Committee.

2021, Dr. Kimmons published his 7th book, "The Personal and Political Life and Legacy" of his adopted godmother, The Honorable Shirley Chisholm.

Dr. Kimmons has been awarded the key to 12 major cities in the United States by the mayors. He was honored and recognized for his community service, civic and leadership contributions in the areas of race relations and community relations.

Dr. Willie J. Kimmons is a religious man, family man, parent of four (4) adult children, two (2) daughters and two (2) sons, all of whom are graduates of Historically and Predominately Black Colleges and Universities (H.B.C.U.'s). Dr. Kimmons dedicated his current book, <u>A Parenting Guidebook</u>, to his seven (7) grandchildren, five (5) girls and two (2) boys.

In the past 5 years, Dr. Kimmons has spoken in 50 cities, signed and sold over 400,000 copies of his Parenting Guidebook. His godmother, the late, great, Honorable Shirley Chisholm, encouraged him to write <u>A Parenting Guidebook</u>. She wrote the foreword to his parenting guidebook.

Dr. Kimmons' interest in education stems from a background of training and experience in the area of human development, leadership, and community service. He is always eager to promote learning and development of the student by setting the atmosphere to motivate not only the student, but also other individuals within the educational arena.

Dr. Willie J. Kimmons has spent his entire career getting to the root of understanding the nature of the issues confronting today's parents, teachers, and students. He has successfully dealt with many of the challenges of human beings throughout his career as a professional educator and community activist. His life's ambition is to expand enthusiasm for education, and continue his commitment and dedication to the learner.

Dr. Kimmons' philosophy is … that institutions should be committed to providing quality educational and health care services and should be held accountable by the communities they serve. He welcomes the challenge of giving and sharing leadership that supports these goals. He further believes that by uniting our energies and supporting our educational and health care systems, we will be able to keep our students academically challenged, and our citizens better prepared for life.

Dr. Kimmons' Motto is …"Help Me to Help Somebody to Save Our Children, and Save Our Schools; Never, Ever, Give Up On Our Children, Because Our Children are Our Greatest Resource; Our Children are an Extension of Us; and Our Children are Our Future."

Dr. Kimmons is a new voice for partners in education. In 2005, he founded his corporation, Save Children Save Schools, Inc. Educational Services.

Contact:
Save Children Save Schools, Inc.
Dr. Willie J. Kimmons
1653 Lawrence Circle
Daytona Beach, FL 32117
Office: 386-253-4920   Cell: 386-451-4780

E-mail: WJKimmons@aol.com

CO AUTHOR

DR. GAYLE INGRAHAM

Motivational Speaker

Community Leader

Trainer

Mental Health Coach

Dr. Gayle Ingraham was born in Nassau Bahamas. At the age of 13, she along with her family moved to Plant City, Florida where she attended Tomlin Middle School and received her high school diploma from Plant City Senior High School. She was a student athlete, secretary for Future Business Leaders of America and served as a Color Guard for Jr. ROTC.

Dr. Ingraham received her undergraduate degree from Florida Metropolitan University, Tampa, Florida in Criminal Justice with a minor in Business Administration. She received a Master's in Educational Leadership degree within 10 months from American Inter-Continental University On-line Program. During this time, Dr. Ingraham was instrumental in establishing several online tutorials for English as a Second Language Learners. In 2014, Dr. Ingraham earned a Doctorate Degree in Educational Leadership from Argosy University, Tampa, Florida. She was one of the founding members of the Psi Beta Delta Honor Society for International Students and served as Vice President for Argosy University Tampa Chapter.

Dr. Ingraham established her non-profit organization EmTim Training & Consulting Services, Inc. (ETCS) in 1999. ETCS provides workshops for case managers, social workers, parents, grandparents, Not for profit board development and program evaluation. Additional training for train the trainer tutors, staff development, management skills, team building, Domestic Violence, CPR and First Aid, life skills, money smarts, dealing with children with difficult behaviors and motivating children to learn.

Dr. Ingraham worked on the Disaster Preparedness Task Force, Washington, DC and was the first train the trainer for Disaster Preparedness with a non-profit organization in Dallas, Texas training 250 employees. Dr. Ingraham has developed curriculum and course catalogs as well as trained teachers and taught English as a Second Language courses to adults, graduating more than 200 students.

While working in Dallas, in 2002, Dr. Ingraham expanded her non-profit organization to assist underserved children from Africa. She tutored over 150 students in reading, reading comprehension, writing, math, basic computer skills, taught infant, child and adult CPR and a variety of workshops including parenting skills, financial management, building healthy relationships, single parenting, and behavior modification.

Dr. Ingraham returned to Florida in 2008. Since her return to Florida, she has been instrumental in developing policies and procedures for faith based and non-profit organizations. Dr. Ingraham's non-profit organization has expanded to include training business consultants, volunteer and mentor training, Leadership skills, and Organizational Management.

Dr. Ingraham has held positons as Human Resource Analyst, Program Director, Social Worker, Counselor, Behavioral Specialist and most recently Program Manager. She served as board member to several not-for-profit organization, volunteered with local schools, and community organizations to bridge the gap between family, community, faith and schools.

EmTim Training & Consulting Services
Dr. Gayle S. Ingraham, CEO/Founder
P. O. Box 1354, Mango, Florida 33550.
Email: 4gayleingraham@gmail.com
Telephone: 813-764-5595
Website: https:\\www.drgayleingraham.com

MODULE ONE

OVERVIEW /INTRODUCTION

The instructors for this course are Dr. Willie Kimmons, who is the author of A Parenting Guidebook and Dr. Gayle Ingraham, Co-Author of Parenting Forever Workbook. Florida Statutes requires that parents who are divorcing must take at least 4 hours of parenting coursework. However, we know that it takes a lifetime to raise children.

This 7 module family interactive workbook is designed for in-home, classroom, or professional setting involving children. We will provide you with the needed tools to share as you work with children and families. Regardless to the role one play in a child's life, a parent or significant adult in the household is one most important person to the child. This workbook will be a great resource to help concerned professionals get through the most critical time in in their workplace. It is a useful tool for counselors, therapists, teachers, case managers, systems navigators and social workers.

This Parenting Forever Interactive Workbook is filled with hands on activities and discussion topics that you can use one-on-one or in group settings. This workbook will encourage you to stay connected to children, grandparents, Kinship caregivers, schools, faith-based and community organizations to help save our children and save our schools.

> The 3 Saturdays required training workshop for parents will be supplemented with a copy of the Parenting Guidebook authored by Dr. Willie J. Greer Kimmons as part of the training.

This Parenting Forever workbook is designed to assist parents, grandparents and significant adults in the household with rearing, supporting and protecting their children. This workbook is to help parents and families to become more active participants in their children's lives.

PARENTING FOREVER GUIDE INTERACTIVE WORKBOOK WITH ACTIVITIES TO DO WITH YOUR FAMILY by Dr. Willie J. Greer Kimmons & Dr. Gayle S. Ingraham

The workbook is designed to form a working relationship/partnership with the Juvenile Justice Systems, Department of Children and Families, State Attorney Offices, and Educational youth programs. The workbook would provide a 3 Saturdays required training program for parents, grandparents or significant adults in the household as a Juvenile Diversion Alternative Program for at-risk youth and communities.

The ultimate intention of the program is to hopefully influence our youth to remain crime free and hold the parents, grandparents or significant adults responsible by requiring them to participate in the 3 Saturdays training program. The program will address behavior problems, developing positives and better attitudes about life, property and community needs, self-respect and responsibilities of the parents on behalf of their children. Extensive counseling and mentoring sessions will be utilized throughout the training program as well as case management services.

Through referrals by the State's Attorney Office, Juvenile Justice Systems and Department of Children and Families, parents and children would be assigned based on the individual needs of the youth. This training program is designed to hold parents accountable for their children's behavior and actions in the communities. Successful completion of this program occurs when the parents, grandparents or significant adult in the home have met the 3 Saturdays requirements and the child has remained crime free.

God didn't make dumb children, he didn't make bad and disobedient children, we as adults, parents and grandparents made our young people this way because children imitate adults behavior, good or bad. This is why this youth diversion program/workbook training is so important to hold our parents accountable.

Raising children can be challenging in many ways. Caring for infants and small children can take quite a bit of time. All of us have heard that it takes a village to raise a child. This is true with patience, love, partnerships and the support of your spouse. Parents are generally responsible for:

- Keeping children safe,
- Listening to children and spending time with them,
- Providing affection, direction and consistency,

PARENTING FOREVER GUIDE INTERACTIVE WORKBOOK WITH ACTIVITIES TO DO WITH YOUR FAMILY by Dr. Willie J. Greer Kimmons & Dr. Gayle S. Ingraham

- Setting and enforcing boundaries for children,
- Monitoring friendships children make and
- Seeking help for any medical or behavioral concerns.

> **"Children are our greatest resource; they are our future and extension of parents." (Kimmons 2012)**

Whether you believe this or not, parenting can be lots of fun. Parenting is about you and your children enjoying the journey together. There will be times when raising children can be challenging. So hang in there, stay focused and be the best role model you can be for your children.

There are seven modules within this workbook.

Upon completion of this course you will have gained more knowledge about parenting and understand the importance of parental involvement in every stage of a child's life.

NOTES:

_____

_____

_____

_____

_____

_____

_____

_____

PARENTING FOREVER INTERACTIVE WORKBOOK TRAINING WILL HELP YOU:

- Be better equipped as your child's first teacher to handle your role as parent.
- Learn effective communication and ways to keep families together.

PARENTING FOREVER GUIDE INTERACTIVE WORKBOOK WITH ACTIVITIES TO DO WITH YOUR FAMILY by Dr. Willie J. Greer Kimmons & Dr. Gayle S. Ingraham

- Understand your role as parents, partners, teachers and case manager that will help you to encourage children's education.
- Learn tips to model when dealing with children's behavior as well as ways to praise and reward children.
- Understand your role in household management – the balance between, work and play.
- Be an advocate to deal with school and community related issues.

NOTES:

_____
_____
_____
_____
_____
_____
_____
_____
_____
_____
_____
_____
_____
_____

LET'S BEGIN

MODULE TWO

RAISING AND COMMUNICATING WITH YOUR CHILDREN, THIS IS PARENTING 101.

Children need support

TOPIC: Parenting

GOALS:

- Understand your role as a parent.
- Increase positive communication with your children.
- Increase the understanding of your responsibility in rearing your children.
- Increase your understanding of your responsibility as your children's responsible adult in rearing your children.

PARENTING FOREVER GUIDE INTERACTIVE WORKBOOK WITH ACTIVITIES TO DO WITH YOUR FAMILY by Dr. Willie J. Greer Kimmons & Dr. Gayle S. Ingraham

NOTES: _____

_____

_____

_____

_____

_____

_____

DISCUSSION: INGRAHAM'S PARENTING STAGES:

Fathers and grandfathers need support

PARENT NEEDS SUPPORT

Parenting is the most important job you will ever have. Parenting can be challenging. Your parenting role will change as your children grow and learn.

Parents who receive help from other parents, mentors in the community, churches, schools, community organizations and other resources can improve parenting skills. Quality parenting requires a lot of support. When parents improve their learning, they can better assist their children academically, financially, socially and spiritually.

PARENTING FOREVER GUIDE INTERACTIVE WORKBOOK WITH ACTIVITIES TO DO WITH YOUR FAMILY by Dr. Willie J. Greer Kimmons & Dr. Gayle S. Ingraham

Good and quality parenting is like building a house on a solid foundation. Unlike houses, children do not come with a blueprint. So, as we raise our children, we are developing the blueprint with them that will impact on their lives forever. We must invest in our children's future.

INGRAHAM'S PARENTING STAGES:

TIP: "Be patient, tolerant and compassionate."
Dr. Willie J. Kimmons

Brotherly Love

Stage One: Ages 0-9 Role Modeling Stage

- Parents should use this opportunity to teach, model and discipline.
- This is the foundation building block stage.
- Use this stage to get children's behavior under control.

Dr. Willie J. Greer Kimmons

PARENTING FOREVER GUIDE INTERACTIVE WORKBOOK WITH ACTIVITIES TO DO WITH YOUR FAMILY by Dr. Willie J. Greer Kimmons & Dr. Gayle S. Ingraham

- At this stage, children should have a good understanding of consequences for their choices.
- Children are watching everything you do and listening to everything you say, so be a good role model and choose your words wisely.

LIST YOUR IDEAS: _____

_____

_____

_____

_____

_____

_____

Stage Two: Ages 10-15 Make-it or Break-it Stage

TIP: Communicating with children is important in this stage. Most children in this age group feel "Sandwiched in". For example, children transiting from elementary to middle school and from middle school to high school. ***Dr. Gayle S. Ingraham***

- The middle school child thinks he/she is too old to do what they did in elementary school.
- They are not old enough to do some things such as go to the movie or ball game by themselves.
- They still depend on parents at this stage for transportation.
- They are curious about dating, sex, drugs and alcohol.
- They want to tell you what to do and can be rebellious at this age.
- At this stage in a child's life, "peer pressure is stronger than parent pressure."

LIST YOUR IDEAS:

_____

_____

_____

_____

PARENTING FOREVER GUIDE INTERACTIVE WORKBOOK WITH ACTIVITIES TO DO WITH YOUR FAMILY by Dr. Willie J. Greer Kimmons & Dr. Gayle S. Ingraham

Stage 3: Ages 15-18 Negotiator/Investigator Stage

The Risk Takers

- Want to exert their independence.
- Have a "Know it All" attitude.
- Want to borrow the car and drive around with friends.
- Want to date, participate in sports and other extra-curricular activities, and focus a great deal of time on social media.
- Begin to prepare for college.
- Work on part time jobs, which provide them a great opportunity to earn some spending money and learn to manage their money and save for the future.

LIST YOUR IDEAS HERE:

_____

_____

_____

_____

_____

_____

Stage 4: Ages 19 and older Coasting Stage

- Many teens/young adults have not moved out due to economic conditions, in college and/or working.
- They might be planning a family or single parents.
- They may need mentorship, advising and financial support.

TIP: Do not be an enabler. It is difficult to watch your children as well as other children go through their growing pains. However, do not get children out of every situation, but coach and advise them. ***Dr. Willie J. Kimmons***

PARENTING FOREVER GUIDE INTERACTIVE WORKBOOK WITH ACTIVITIES TO DO WITH YOUR FAMILY by Dr. Willie J. Greer Kimmons & Dr. Gayle S. Ingraham

LIST YOUR IDEAS:

_____

_____

_____

_____

_____

_____

Discussion: Role of Parents

DIRECTIONS: In <u>The Parenting Guidebook</u> "Role of Parents" on page: Pg. 35 read the 12 roles of parents and discuss each one.

Role of Parents Discussion Notes:

_____

_____

_____

_____

_____

_____

_____

_____

_____

_____

_____

_____

_____

PARENTING FOREVER GUIDE INTERACTIVE WORKBOOK WITH ACTIVITIES TO DO WITH YOUR FAMILY by Dr. Willie J. Greer Kimmons & Dr. Gayle S. Ingraham

TIP: Children ask many questions. Inquiring minds want to know! Everyone involved (pastor, teacher, case managers, counselors, grandparents, significant adults in the household, parents, social workers, therapists), should answer questions honestly. If you are not sure what the answer is, spend time searching for answers in the dictionary, encyclopedia and web searches with your children. Always remember, there is no right or wrong way in raising children. Be sure you are consistent and persistent when solving problems with children. ***Dr. Willie J. Kimmons***

Vacation time

TIP: "Parents took us everywhere we needed to go such as school, church and sports events. Our parents knew everyone in the community. The community helped raise children that lived within the community." Dr. Willie J. Kimmons

PARENTING FOREVER GUIDE INTERACTIVE WORKBOOK WITH ACTIVITIES TO DO WITH YOUR FAMILY by Dr. Willie J. Greer Kimmons & Dr. Gayle S. Ingraham

LIST 2-3 WAYS WE CAN KEEP OUR CHILDREN SAFE:

1. _____
   _____
   _____

2. _____
   _____
   _____

3. _____
   _____
   _____

Activity: Role of Parents

1. Share ideas of how each of you has spent time with your children:

   _____
   _____
   _____
   _____
   _____
   _____

2. What does it mean to provide affection, discipline and consistency?

   _____
   _____

Grand parenting

3. How do you set and enforce limits for children?

   _____
   _____

PARENTING FOREVER GUIDE INTERACTIVE WORKBOOK WITH ACTIVITIES TO DO WITH
YOUR FAMILY by Dr. Willie J. Greer Kimmons & Dr. Gayle S. Ingraham

4. Do you know who your children's friends are? List their names:

   _____

   _____

5. How do you monitor their friendship with others especially their social media
   presence and activities?

   _____

   _____

6. How do you talk with your child about health and behavioral concerns?

   _____

   _____

7. Do you have rules at home? If so, please share:

   _____

   _____

8. What is the basic problem that faces parents today?

   _____

   _____

9. What routines do you and your children share together?

   _____

   _____

PARENTING FOREVER GUIDE INTERACTIVE WORKBOOK WITH ACTIVITIES TO DO WITH YOUR FAMILY by Dr. Willie J. Greer Kimmons & Dr. Gayle S. Ingraham

Activity: Good Communication

ACTIVITY	IDEAS ON HOW TO ACCOMPLISH EACH
Praying with your child and attending church with your child/ children	Example: Saying prayers before bed, blessing food before eating.
Sharing an experience, event or activity with a child/children	
Hugs to and from your child/ children	
Talking with your child/children	
Listening to your child/children	
Support your child/children with after school activities	
Best friends/True friends	
Participating in teen-aged child/ children's work and life skills development	
Attending school activities with your child/children	
Reading to and with your child/ children	
Telling your child that you love him/her	

PARENTING FOREVER GUIDE INTERACTIVE WORKBOOK WITH ACTIVITIES TO DO WITH
YOUR FAMILY by Dr. Willie J. Greer Kimmons & Dr. Gayle S. Ingraham

Spending Time with your child/children	
Share memories with your child/children	
Share values with your child/children	
Share love of Learning with your child/children	
Discussion: Experience and Exposure	
Share sense of Humor	

PARENTING FOREVER GUIDE INTERACTIVE WORKBOOK WITH ACTIVITIES TO DO WITH YOUR FAMILY by Dr. Willie J. Greer Kimmons & Dr. Gayle S. Ingraham

Topic: Tips for Good Communication

DIRECTIONS: On page 49 in <u>A Parenting Guidebook</u>, review and discuss tips for "GOOD COMMUNICATION". List a few of the tips that are important to you and that you will use immediately to improve communication with your child/children.

Always treat children with courtesy, kindness and respect.

Example: Avoidance of cursing and name calling

- _____
  _____
  _____

Listen actively by repeating your child's feelings with empathy and understanding.

- _____
  _____
  _____

Avoid misunderstandings by seeking to understand your child's idea. (Reflective listening)

- _____
  _____
  _____

PARENTING FOREVER GUIDE INTERACTIVE WORKBOOK WITH ACTIVITIES TO DO WITH YOUR FAMILY by Dr. Willie J. Greer Kimmons & Dr. Gayle S. Ingraham

Activity: Tips for Good Communication

DIRECTIONS: On page 49 in <u>A Parenting Guidebook</u>, review and discuss tips for "GOOD COMMUNICATION". List a few of the tips that are important to you and that you will use immediately to improve communication with your child/children.

Cool off before you talk, and choose your words carefully.

- _____
  _____
  _____

Remember, if you want to be heard, you first must be available and listen.

- _____
  _____
  _____

Listen more and talk less.

- _____
  _____
  _____

While listening, don't mentally rehearse your reply.

- _____
  _____
  _____

Use plenty of "me and you" messages.

PARENTING FOREVER GUIDE INTERACTIVE WORKBOOK WITH ACTIVITIES TO DO WITH YOUR FAMILY by Dr. Willie J. Greer Kimmons & Dr. Gayle S. Ingraham

Directions: Provide examples.

When you _____,

me and you feel_____,

and me and you wish _____.

DIRECTIONS: Below in the chart, work with your children (child) to list ways that you communicate with them. Make a note of your child/children's responses or comments children made.

TOPIC YOU DISCUSSED WITH YOUR CHILDREN	LIST YOUR CHILDREN'S REPONSE	LIST WHAT YOU CAN DO DIFFERENTLY

MODULE THREE

THE ROLE OF PARENTS IN REARING CHILDREN

*Topic: **Dealing with Children's Behaviors***

GOALS:

Family game day

- Increase your understanding of what you can do or what you have already done to be a positive role model for your children.
- Understand how your behavior impacts your children's behavior.
- Increase your understanding of empathy towards your children while disciplining them.
- Increase your knowledge of at least 8 problem solving strategies that you can use to effectively solve problems with your child/children

Parents are children's first teachers. Children model what they see their parents do. We can spend time telling them what they are doing wrong, but parents must be positive role models for their children at all times. Some days, parenting is much difficult than others. Just when you think you have everything under control something happens unexpectedly. For example, your children missed the school bus, the car had a flat tire, or one of the children is ill requiring you to take a day from work to be with them.

PARENTING FOREVER GUIDE INTERACTIVE WORKBOOK WITH ACTIVITIES TO DO WITH YOUR FAMILY by Dr. Willie J. Greer Kimmons & Dr. Gayle S. Ingraham

> TIP: Always remember… Good parents are not perfect. Do not allow distractions to overtake you. Use these distractions as an opportunity to grow everyday.
> **Dr. Gayle Ingraham**

> DIRECTIONS: In <u>A Parenting Guidebook</u> on page 23, we learned that it is important for parents to get involved in their children's education. Experts agree that the following are benefits of parental involvement.

List them:

1. _____
   _____
   _____
   _____

2. _____
   _____
   _____
   _____

3. _____
   _____
   _____
   _____

4. _____
   _____
   _____
   _____

PARENTING FOREVER GUIDE INTERACTIVE WORKBOOK WITH ACTIVITIES TO DO WITH YOUR FAMILY by Dr. Willie J. Greer Kimmons & Dr. Gayle S. Ingraham

Topic: Role Modeling

> *DIRECTIONS: In The Parenting Guidebook on page 27:*

THE BEST ROLE MODEL FOR YOUR CHILD IS:_____

Remember that all children learn differently. Parents are children's first teachers. Children model what they see you do. You can spend time telling them what they are doing wrong, but if you are not doing the right thing with them, it is difficult for them to respect you.

List 3 standard modalities (the way something exists or is done) of learning: (Pg. 24)

1. _____
2. _____
3. _____

When parents are positively involved with their children from birth, children are better ready for school. When parents take the time to help them with school work and play time, children get excited about learning.

NOTES:

PARENTING FOREVER GUIDE INTERACTIVE WORKBOOK WITH ACTIVITIES TO DO WITH YOUR FAMILY by Dr. Willie J. Greer Kimmons & Dr. Gayle S. Ingraham

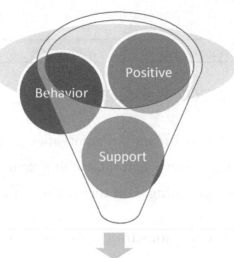

Focus on desired behaviors

Behavior Types	Tips for Desired Behavior	What makes it worse
Positive Behavior (this is the type of behavior every parent wants from their children)	Model the behavior. Give attention to the positive behavior. Reward, Praise, Celebrate.	Ignoring children when they are doing the right thing. Not taking the time to celebrate them.
Aggravating Behavior (type of behavior you want to minimize or put a stop to as quickly as possible)	Set the expectations. Be firm with decisions. Help child to understand consequences for choices.	Giving too much attention. Changing your mind about your discipline decision.
Negative Behavior (type of behavior you want to get rid of immediately)	Set expectations immediately. Punishment/consequences such as contracts, privilege taken away, favorite game/toy taken away.	Ignoring, becoming aggressive (screaming, arguing back with the child) Taking frustration out on the other children.

PARENTING FOREVER GUIDE INTERACTIVE WORKBOOK WITH ACTIVITIES TO DO WITH YOUR FAMILY by Dr. Willie J. Greer Kimmons & Dr. Gayle S. Ingraham

DIRECTIONS: In <u>The Parenting Guidebook</u>, read last paragraph on pg. 40 "Quality parenting can save our children......" Fill in the blank for each word or words below:

1. Higher_____
2. Better _____
3. Stronger Language _____
4. Improved_____
5. Pride and_____

Make sports fun

TAKE NOTES HERE:

_____
_____
_____
_____
_____
_____
_____
_____
_____
_____
_____

TIP: When parents spend time with their children, the results can be incredible. *Dr. Willie J. Kimmons*

PARENTING FOREVER GUIDE INTERACTIVE WORKBOOK WITH ACTIVITIES TO DO WITH YOUR FAMILY by Dr. Willie J. Greer Kimmons & Dr. Gayle S. Ingraham

Topic: Planning Activity for Rewards

Sometimes it can be challenging to get your children to:

- Engage in school work.
- Complete their homework assignments.
- Get involved in after school activities.
- Complete tasks on time.
- Limit their social media use.

TIP: Disciplining children can be challenging. We can motivate children by focusing on true encouraging words. Children need to be motivated from the inside out. What they really feel will be shown through their actions. Encouraging words motivate a child to learn and to make good choices. ***Dr. Willie J. Kimmons***

NOTES:

_____

_____

_____

_____

_____

_____

_____

_____

_____

_____

PARENTING FOREVER GUIDE INTERACTIVE WORKBOOK WITH ACTIVITIES TO DO WITH YOUR FAMILY by Dr. Willie J. Greer Kimmons & Dr. Gayle S. Ingraham

> DIRECTIONS: Choose rewards, write them or use the form below to create your own reward ideas.

Decide behaviors to increase:

_____

_____

_____

_____

_____

Most children generally want to please their parents and their teachers. Children respond well when adults praise their efforts.

SOCIAL SKILLS REWARDS:

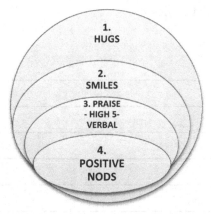

1. HUGS
2. SMILES
3. PRAISE - HIGH 5- VERBAL
4. POSITIVE NODS

NOTES:_____

_____

_____

_____

_____

_____

_____

_____

_____

PARENTING FOREVER GUIDE INTERACTIVE WORKBOOK WITH ACTIVITIES TO DO WITH YOUR FAMILY by Dr. Willie J. Greer Kimmons & Dr. Gayle S. Ingraham

Stars

- Points
- Tokens
- Symbols
- Coupons
- Happy face

Educational field trip

REWARD CHARTS/CONTRACTS (Ages 9-13)

- Healthy snack items such as fruit or yogurt.
- Watch their favorite movie/TV show.
- Games.
- Breakfast, lunch or dinner at a favorite restaurant.
- Educational Computer Games.

NOTES:_____

_____

_____

_____

_____

_____

_____

_____

_____

_____

PARENTING FOREVER GUIDE INTERACTIVE WORKBOOK WITH ACTIVITIES TO DO WITH YOUR FAMILY by Dr. Willie J. Greer Kimmons & Dr. Gayle S. Ingraham

> TIP: Chores, contracts and rewards should be given based on child/children's age.
> ## Dr. Gayle Ingraham

Work with each child to create age appropriate chart using some of the ideas below. You can also find chore/reward charts in the office or school supply sections of most stores.

Spending time away from the television

NOTES:_____
_____
_____
_____
_____
_____
_____
_____
_____
_____
_____
_____

CLEAN ROOM	TAKE OUT GARBAGE	SET THE TABLE	FOLD TOWELS	HELP PREPARE DINNER	CLEAN THE BATHROOM	WRITE GROCERY LIST
WASH DISHES	BAKE DESSERT	MAKE ICE TEA	MOP THE KITCHEN FLOOR	VACUUM THE DEN	SWEEP THE FRONT PORCH	DUST FURNITURE
WASH YOUR FACE	BRUSH YOUR TEETH	GO TO BED ON TIME	PUT TOYS AWAY	PUT BIKE AWAY	DO HOMEWORK	HELP WITH YARD WORK

PARENTING FOREVER GUIDE INTERACTIVE WORKBOOK WITH ACTIVITIES TO DO WITH YOUR FAMILY by Dr. Willie J. Greer Kimmons & Dr. Gayle S. Ingraham

Topic: Chore Chart for 2-8 year olds

TIP: Children ages 2-6 may struggle with reading. Consider using both words and pictures to support their confidence to read and work with each child on their reward chart. **Dr. Gayle S. Ingraham**

DIRECTIONS: Practice creating chart using form below.

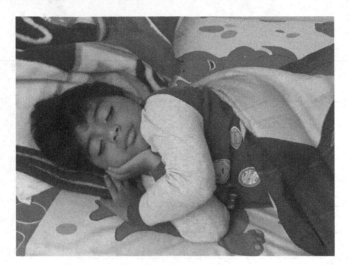

Put kids to bed as scheduled

Chore Chart for 2-8 year olds

CHORE	MONDAY	TUESDAY	WEDNESDAY	THRUSDAY	FRIDAY

PARENTING FOREVER GUIDE INTERACTIVE WORKBOOK WITH ACTIVITIES TO DO WITH YOUR FAMILY by Dr. Willie J. Greer Kimmons & Dr. Gayle S. Ingraham

Discipline with love

Topic: Pre-Teen Talk

Before rewarding your child, here are a few things you should do to make the reward count:

- Discuss with your child what things they want and like. You can easily do so by creating a list of items for them to choose from.
- Discuss with your child the length of time he/she has to display desired behavior before earning rewards.
- Give reward after the positive behavior occurs and on time as scheduled.
- Discuss consequences for choices – good or bad. (withhold reward if desired behavior does not occur).
- Be consistent with giving rewards for the desired behavior.
- What activities/chores you would like your child to do?
- What activities your child looks forward to.
- Look for ways to combine what your child wants and what you want.

PARENTING FOREVER GUIDE INTERACTIVE WORKBOOK WITH ACTIVITIES TO DO WITH YOUR FAMILY by Dr. Willie J. Greer Kimmons & Dr. Gayle S. Ingraham

- Make sure that the activities/chores are age appropriate.
- Praise child (hugs, hand shake, high-fives, etc.) when giving the reward.
- Monitor rewards to see when to change. Sometimes children need to be challenged with new rewards and new ideas.

Activity: Pre-Teen Talk

> DIRECTIONS: Use the chart below to create a reward chart for your pre-teen.

What to do	SUN	MON	TUE	WED	THUR	FRI	SAT
Morning							
Evening							
Before Bed							

Rewards: _____

_____

_____

_____

Consequences: _____

_____

_____

_____   _____

CHILD'S SIGNATURE/DATE   PARENT'S SIGNATURE/DATE

PARENTING FOREVER GUIDE INTERACTIVE WORKBOOK WITH ACTIVITIES TO DO WITH YOUR FAMILY by Dr. Willie J. Greer Kimmons & Dr. Gayle S. Ingraham

Topic: **TEENTALK: SETTING EXPECTATIONS**

DIRECTIONS: Read the last paragraph on page 41 of <u>A Parenting Guidebook</u> starting with: "I am the oldest of 27 sisters and brothers…" After reading this paragraph, discuss parenting support and values ~ what do you still value today.

NOTES:_____

_____

_____

_____

_____

_____

_____

_____

_____

TIPS: Setting expectations is like setting goals for you and your child/children to ensure they are successful.

Check yourself….make sure you are having a good day – sometimes we take out our frustrations on others, which is not fair.

Make sure that the child is having a good day as well – so that he/she will be excited that you are showing some interest in what they are doing.
Dr. Gayle Ingraham

1. ***Watch your tone:*** Screaming frustrates the situation. "Do unto others as you would have them do unto you".
2. ***Do not intimidate:*** You are much bigger than your child. When you intimidate children, they might rebel at times. Treat your children fairly.
3. ***Set realistic expectations:*** As you communicate with your child, make sure that the child understands your expectations.

Dr. Willie J. Greer Kimmons

PARENTING FOREVER GUIDE INTERACTIVE WORKBOOK WITH ACTIVITIES TO DO WITH YOUR FAMILY by Dr. Willie J. Greer Kimmons & Dr. Gayle S. Ingraham

4. ***Make sure your expectations are clear:*** Do not give them a laundry list of items to do. Let them participate in the activity of setting expectations.

5. ***Developmentally Appropriate***: You know your children best. For example, a child could be 8 but has the ability of a 10-12 year old or a child could be 8 but functions as a 5-7 year old.

6. ***Listen for understanding:*** provide some time during the planning stage to listen to what the child is saying. You may need to write the contract or expectations in simple terms so that the child can read it and understand it.

7. **Mutual:** Make sure that you and the child agree to the expectations.

8. **Write them down:**
   a. You and your child can create a contract which will spell out what he/she will be responsible for, consequences/rewards as well as what the parent will be responsible for and rewards/discipline.
   b. Contracts are important – you or your child may forget – especially over time.
   c. Contracts can be displayed in room – on bedroom or closet door.

9. ***Meet and discuss weekly:*** Set a day each week that you have agreed to meet with your child to discuss. For example you may meet with one child Mondays after school and another Tuesday after school. You can limit the time – for example, 30 minutes. The child gets to share 15 minutes then you share for 15 minutes.
   a. Speak positively about your child's progress
   b. Discipline can be positive – not always negative – you want it to be a memorable moment so that the children learn from his/her mistakes.

NOTES:_____

_____

_____

_____

_____

_____

_____

PARENTING FOREVER GUIDE INTERACTIVE WORKBOOK WITH ACTIVITIES TO DO WITH YOUR FAMILY by Dr. Willie J. Greer Kimmons & Dr. Gayle S. Ingraham

> TIP: Remember, just because a child is 17 years old does not make them responsible for babysitting, cooking, cleaning and other chores if you have not prepared them.
> *Dr. Gayle S. Ingraham*

> DIRECTIONS: Here are a few typical things teens deal with —let's talk about how we should address each.

Child's issue	Ideas on how to resolve
Alcohol/Drug Use	• Set clear expectations. • Educate yourself on the type of drug/alcohol your child is using. • Get your child help as soon as possible. • Educate yourself. • Attend support group such as narcotic. anonymous or alcohol anonymous.
Sex	• Talks with your child about birth control/protecting themselves. • Encourage sex education classes through reputable organizations such as hospitals. • Discuss responsibilities such as pregnancy, employment, becoming a mother/father. • Create a shopping list of items that an infant will need with your child. Take them to the store and have them locate these items and cost associated with each item.

PARENTING FOREVER GUIDE INTERACTIVE WORKBOOK WITH ACTIVITIES TO DO WITH YOUR FAMILY by Dr. Willie J. Greer Kimmons & Dr. Gayle S. Ingraham

I want a Car/ I want my own apartment	• Discuss what type of car/apartment child wants. • Discuss budget associated with each. • Discuss employment/saving for what period of time in order to accomplish the goal. • Have child attend life skills classes associated with independent living or spend time educating them yourself. • Allow you children to dream – don't discourage them from dreaming. Children don't always understand cost associated with an item that they want – that's why it is important that we take the time to educate them.
Teen loses cell phone for the 2nd time	• Have the teen work to earn extra money to save for another cell phone. • Chores: yard work, babysitting, part time job at a local supermarket.
Teen misses curfew	• Cut the curfew short by the same amount of time that he/she is late.
Teen failed to follow directions	• Write a list of instructions for your child to follow – once child shared that he/she has completed the task, you can review and discuss. If child has done what was required – praise him/her. If he/she did not – talk about it and repeat the steps again. • Another suggestion is to give them a recipe to follow by themselves. Such as baking a cake, making salad, washing, rinsing and drying dishes, doing laundry.
I forgot to do it	• Have child write notes and post it for reminders. • If the child has a cell phone, have them set alarms, make a schedule with reminders.

PARENTING FOREVER GUIDE INTERACTIVE WORKBOOK WITH ACTIVITIES TO DO WITH YOUR FAMILY by Dr. Willie J. Greer Kimmons & Dr. Gayle S. Ingraham

NOTES:_____

_____

_____

_____

_____

_____

_____

_____

_____

_____

Discussion: Teen Talk SETTING EXPECTATIONS

DIRECTIONS: In A Parenting Guidebook, pg. 69, read "The Power of Grandparents" and discuss the following and chat about how you think your child/children would answer these questions.

Grandparents ask direct, point-blank, embarrassing questions that parents are too nervous to ask:

- "Who's the girl/boy?"
- "How come you're doing poorly in history?"
- "Why are your eyes always red?"
- "Did you go to the doctor? What did the doctor say?"

What other questions may a grandparent ask and why?

_____

_____

_____

_____

_____

_____

_____

_____

PARENTING FOREVER GUIDE INTERACTIVE WORKBOOK WITH ACTIVITIES TO DO WITH YOUR FAMILY by Dr. Willie J. Greer Kimmons & Dr. Gayle S. Ingraham

Topic: Parent/Child Agreement

- For children age 10 and older, consider writing a simple Parent/Child Agreement. This tool is a great way for older children to understand consequences for choices.
- Many times children would remember what was agreed on more often than you will. This agreement is a simple way to avoid any conflicts or misunderstanding as to what the desired behavior is and the award for each.
- This agreement can be simple, bulleted and placed on the back of your child's bedroom door so that he/she can see it as a reminder.
- The agreement should have a space for both child and parent's signatures including start and end dates.

(See a sample of Parent/Child Agreement on the next page.)

NOTES:_____

_____

_____

_____

_____

_____

_____

_____

_____

_____

PARENTING FOREVER GUIDE INTERACTIVE WORKBOOK WITH ACTIVITIES TO DO WITH YOUR FAMILY by Dr. Willie J. Greer Kimmons & Dr. Gayle S. Ingraham

PARENT/CHILD AGREEMENT

Both child and parent should be in agreement about each item and the consequences/rewards as they appear on the agreement:

What will the child do/by what date:

_____

What did you and your child agree that he/she will do	By what date	Earned Privilege/ Reward

Decide together the consequence for not completing the contract?

_____
_____
_____
_____
_____

_____   _____
Child's Signature   Parent Signature

Expiration date for Agreement: _____

PARENTING FOREVER GUIDE INTERACTIVE WORKBOOK WITH ACTIVITIES TO DO WITH YOUR FAMILY by Dr. Willie J. Greer Kimmons & Dr. Gayle S. Ingraham

Topic: Make Rewards Count~ Model the Behavior

GIVE INSTRUCTIONS – SHORT ~ CLEAR~ TO THE POINT

- Before you give the instruction, think about and process in your mind exactly what you want to say.
- Minimize distractions for yourself and the child before giving instructions (e.g. turn music, cell phone, TV and video games off).
- Call the child by name. (not frustrated or with an angry voice)
- Get down on the child's level and make eye contact/ sit together.
- Use a soft firm voice (not frustrated or with an angry voice).
- Be clear about what you expect the child to do.
- Give instructions one step at a time.
- Repeat what you expect the child to do and ask the child to repeat it back to you.
- Ask if they understand the instructions.
- State the instruction as an instruction not a favor, in question form or as a request.
- Praise and reward as soon as the child follows the instructions.
- Support your instruction with consequences for the choice. Never tell a child what you will or will not do without following through.

Assign age
appropriate chores

PARENTING FOREVER GUIDE INTERACTIVE WORKBOOK WITH ACTIVITIES TO DO WITH YOUR FAMILY by Dr. Willie J. Greer Kimmons & Dr. Gayle S. Ingraham

GIVE INSTRUCTIONS – SHORT ~ CLEAR~ TO THE POINT

ANNOYING BEHAVIORS:

Annoying behaviors, such as crying, pouting, whining can be dealt with by a period of ignoring the behavior and giving a "straight to the point" direction.

Write an example of what you will say to your child who is exhibiting annoying behaviors:

We play together and
share our toys.

_____

_____

_____

_____

_____

_____

_____

_____

_____

Let's Discuss:

Discuss annoying behaviors that you will ignore for a short period of time, prior to giving "straight to the point" directions:

1. _____

2. _____

3. _____

4. _____

PARENTING FOREVER GUIDE INTERACTIVE WORKBOOK WITH ACTIVITIES TO DO WITH YOUR FAMILY by Dr. Willie J. Greer Kimmons & Dr. Gayle S. Ingraham

MISBEHAVING BEHAVIORS:

Misbehaving behaviors such as, not following directions, stamping feet, and tantrums can really get both you and your child upset.

Write a sentence or discuss how you will deal with your child/children who are exhibiting this type of

Take time to be creative.

behavior: _____

_____

_____

TIP: Decide before you speak as to what you will say to your child; use a calm voice (inside voice, give directions, explain the consequence for choices). *Dr. Gayle S. Ingraham*

List a few ways you can handle your child's misbehaviors:

1. _____
2. _____
3. _____
4. _____

GIVING INSTRUCTIONS – SHORT ~ CLEAR~ TO THE POINT

DOWN TIME:

TIP: Taking privileges away from children should be the last resort. The down time should not always be negative. **Dr. Gayle S. Ingraham**

PARENTING FOREVER GUIDE INTERACTIVE WORKBOOK WITH ACTIVITIES TO DO WITH YOUR FAMILY by Dr. Willie J. Greer Kimmons & Dr. Gayle S. Ingraham

ROLE PLAY ACTIVITY #1 Discuss how you will handle this situation.

> Mark, age 7 and Betty age 6 are fighting in the den and broke the remote control for the television. You later discovered the broken remote and asked what happened and who broke the remote. Both Mark and Betty blamed each other for the broken remote.

PARENT: (Phone rings, you answer and it is one of your friends. Both Mark and Betty are in the same room where you answer the phone).

PARENT: *"You will not believe what happened today. My honest and awesome kids broke the remote and could you believe they stood in front of my face and lied about what happened. Let me tell you how I found out. I was cleaning the den and moved the chair to vacuum under it and out fell the remote, which was broken into 50 pieces. Can you believe this?"*

ROLE PLAY ACTIVITY #2 Discuss how you will handle this situation.

> Your 16 year old is arguing with you, cursing at you and tells you how much he/she hates you because you will not buy him/her the cell phone he/she wants. The 16 year old tells you that they could hardly wait to leave your house "for good."

PARENT: *"You will not disrespect me like that".* Who do you think you are that you would speak to me in that manner? If you think you are grown, pack your bags and leave…. Who cares!" (You walk away and for the rest of the evening, regardless to what he/she says, you ignored them.)

NOTES:_____

_____

_____

_____

_____

_____

_____

PARENTING FOREVER GUIDE INTERACTIVE WORKBOOK WITH ACTIVITIES TO DO WITH YOUR FAMILY by Dr. Willie J. Greer Kimmons & Dr. Gayle S. Ingraham

Remember:

- The reward must be something that the child likes and age appropriate. For example for younger children the rewards can be stickers, books or a small toy.
- The reward should be something that can be easily taken away by you.
- When you take the reward away, make the down time for no more than 24-48 hours. This time frame is most effective.
- Explain to the child why you are giving them the down time.

Best friends forever

- If the child continues with problem behavior, you should take an additional privilege away from them.
- When giving child down time, make sure that you are calm and not frustrated. Make sure that the behavior matches the consequence.

PARENTING FOREVER GUIDE INTERACTIVE WORKBOOK WITH ACTIVITIES TO DO WITH YOUR FAMILY by Dr. Willie J. Greer Kimmons & Dr. Gayle S. Ingraham

Topic: What Children Need A-Z

DIRECTIONS: In <u>A Parenting Guidebook</u> pg. 219, review "What Children Need from A to Z.

Approval   Brain Power
Caring   Discipline
Education   Friends
Generosity   Hugs
Instruction   Joy
Kisses   Love
Mentors   Naps
Openness   Play Time
Quiet Time   Restrictions
Security   Truth
Understanding   Variety
Welcome   eXercise
Yearning   Zeal

Aunts have rules too!

NOTES:

_____
_____
_____
_____
_____
_____

PARENTING FOREVER GUIDE INTERACTIVE WORKBOOK WITH ACTIVITIES TO DO WITH YOUR FAMILY by Dr. Willie J. Greer Kimmons & Dr. Gayle S. Ingraham

SET EXPECTATIONS

Things to remember!

1. Watch your tone
2. Do not intimidate
3. Set realistic expectations
4. Make your expectations clear
5. Set developmentally appropriate expectations
6. Listen for understanding
7. Make expectations mutual
8. Write them down
9. Meet and discuss weekly

Adapted from: Dr. Gayle Ingraham 2003 parenting training workshop materials

MODULE FOUR

THE ROLE OF FAMILY IN REARING CHILDREN

GOALS:

- Increase your knowledge about the importance of family and family members support.
- Learn a few interesting facts about your family dynamics.
- Understand how to engage family members and significant adults in a fun loving way.
- Understand the power of grand-parenting.

For the purpose of this workbook, family is defined as those adults related to the child or children by blood or marriage. Sisters, brothers and extended family play an important role in helping you to raise children.

Other adults such as church family, Sunday School Teachers, Pastors, Choir Directors, Neighbors, Day Care Providers, Teachers, Godparents, and Coaches are individuals who have spent time with your children. They can also help to support you as you raise your children.

| In <u>A Parenting Guidebook:</u> Read the statement by Dr. Teresa Langston on pg. 65. |

How many of you feel the same way that the woman described felt?

_____

Why did she think that her family life would gradually disappear?

_____

Based on the information provided in this paragraph, what are some things this woman can do?

_____

PARENTING FOREVER GUIDE INTERACTIVE WORKBOOK WITH ACTIVITIES TO DO WITH YOUR FAMILY by Dr. Willie J. Greer Kimmons & Dr. Gayle S. Ingraham

Topic: The Power of Grandparents

TIP: Parenting is not a dress rehearsal. The life you live is all there is for you and your children. Parents must be careful how you address behavior patterns in the early stages of your child's life. Children watch everything we say or do. They are consistently watching us.

Dr. Willie Kimmons

Bonding time with my great-grandpa   **Sharing secrets with my great-grandma**

DIRECTIONS: In <u>A Parenting Guidebook</u> on page 69 "THE POWER OF GRANDPARENTS" first paragraph…. Grandparents ask direct, point-blank, embarrassing questions that parents are too nervous to ask. List and discuss them:

1. _____

2. _____

3. _____

4. _____

PARENTING FOREVER GUIDE INTERACTIVE WORKBOOK WITH ACTIVITIES TO DO WITH YOUR FAMILY by Dr. Willie J. Greer Kimmons & Dr. Gayle S. Ingraham

Topic: INTERESTING FACTS

1. The average age of first time drug use among teens is: _____

2. Some   children   start   at   the   age of: _____

3. One out of _____ American children between the ages of _____ and _____ is offered _____ drugs by adults. _____% of these children receives the offer from a _____ and _____% named a _____member as their source.

4. _____drugs can be linked to the increased violence, poor performance in _____, AIDS, birth defects, drug-related crimes, and _____.

ACTIVITY: **Interesting Facts** after reading A Parenting Guidebook page 69 last section, "As grandparents, you hold a special place….." please fill in the blanks.

NOTES:

_____
_____
_____
_____
_____
_____
_____
_____
_____

PARENTING FOREVER GUIDE INTERACTIVE WORKBOOK WITH ACTIVITIES TO DO WITH YOUR FAMILY by Dr. Willie J. Greer Kimmons & Dr. Gayle S. Ingraham

Topic: Role Play Activities

> Your 18 year old is leaving the house 2 of his/her friends who you suspect aren't good company for your child. One of the children was arrested several times for possession of drugs and the other for violation of probation.

PARENT: *(Screaming) "Look, I told you that you can't go. You are going to have to break my door down and get through me to get out of here, and believe me, it will not be easy."*

How should this problem be resolved or addressed?

IDEA:

ROLE PLAY SOME OF THE ACTIVITIES LISTED IN <u>A PARENTING GUIDEBOOK (pages 70-71; 79-89)</u>

Here are the topics to choose from:

- Making Home a Positive Place pg. 70
- Laugh Often pg. 71
- Quick Tips pg. 79
- Other Ways to simply Have Fun pg. 80-81
- Plan a Family Day (pg. 82-85)
- Dinner themes (pg. 83)
- Interactive Recipes (pg. 84)
- Dinner Table topics (pg. 85)
- Family Calendar (pg. 85)
- Family Day (Pg. 86-87)

PARENTING FOREVER GUIDE INTERACTIVE WORKBOOK WITH ACTIVITIES TO DO WITH YOUR FAMILY by Dr. Willie J. Greer Kimmons & Dr. Gayle S. Ingraham

Topic: Indoor Picnic

> Parents who care are always seeking to find effective ways to help their children to develop in a manner that they should. The most important thing we can offer our children is love, moral values, a sense of responsibility, hard work and self-respect.
> *Dr. Willie J. Greer Kimmons*

> DIRECTIONS: Use Planning Sheet to assist participants with these activities. Have them work in table groups using the planning sheet to create their activity.

- Get family together to discuss indoor picnic idea.
- Ask the children.
- Ask the children ideas as to what they would like to bring to the family picnic.
- Family members can work together to create a menu including drinks.
- All family members should chip in to help with planning.
- Designate a spot in the home.
- If they are old enough, let them help with meal planning and picnic setup.
- Give each child an assigned task.

PLANNING FAMILY ACTIVITY

> DIRECTIONS: Review topics in <u>A Parenting Guidebook,</u> pages 70-71 and 79-89. Select your topic and let's start planning:

Family fun night

PARENTING FOREVER GUIDE INTERACTIVE WORKBOOK WITH ACTIVITIES TO DO WITH YOUR FAMILY by Dr. Willie J. Greer Kimmons & Dr. Gayle S. Ingraham

What topic did you select? _____
_____
_____

What supplies will you need?
_____
_____
_____

Who will take the lead with the project?
_____

What time will this project take place in the home?
_____

What steps will you take to complete your family activity?
_____
_____
_____

ACTIVITY: Indoor Picnic

> TIP: If you do not have money to purchase picnic items for your family, plan a picnic with the meal prepared for dinner that night "picnic style". ***Dr. Gayle S. Ingraham***

Items needed for this activity:

- Container large enough to put food items in such as:
- Picnic basket, wagon, laundry basket, large shopping bags, large hand bags.
- Beach towel, bed sheet or blanket – to lie on floor – enough for family to sit together (in a circle usually works best).
- Paper plates and napkins.
- Plastic cups, spoons, forks.

PARENTING FOREVER GUIDE INTERACTIVE WORKBOOK WITH ACTIVITIES TO DO WITH YOUR FAMILY by Dr. Willie J. Greer Kimmons & Dr. Gayle S. Ingraham

Excited about family time

ACTIVITIES TO DO WITH YOUR FAMILY: Choose at least two activities to do with your family this week. In the book <u>A Parenting Guidebook</u> several activities are listed that you and your family can participate in. Let's review ideas on pages 70-71, 79-89.

PARENTING FOREVER GUIDE INTERACTIVE WORKBOOK WITH ACTIVITIES TO DO WITH YOUR FAMILY by Dr. Willie J. Greer Kimmons & Dr. Gayle S. Ingraham

ACTIVITY: Remember

There is so much to learn about parenting and as confusing as things can be at times, your best reward is to do the best you can with your children. Remember "children are our future……". So as you continue to raise your children always remember that what you say and do have a lifelong effect on your children. Discipline and communicate with much love.

Activity: Remember (pg. 59)

If you want an honest child, be an

_____ parent.

If you want a kind and fair child, be a

_____ and _____

parent.

If you want a friendly child, be a

_____ parent.

If you want a clean child, be a

_____ Parent

If you want a happy loving child, be a _____ _____

parent.

Learn something new

NOTES:

_____

_____

_____

_____

_____

_____

_____

_____

MODULE FIVE

THE ROLE OF TEACHERS IN REARING CHILDREN

GOALS:

- Increase my knowledge about ways I can support my children's learning
- Increase my knowledge about the Role of Teachers in rearing children so that I can support my children and their school.
- Increase my understanding about what resources are available for me and my children at their schools.

Balancing school and work can be challenging for parent, child and teachers. Parents should begin at an early age educating their children. By the time your child is at the age of 4, he/she should have gained some basic knowledge from parents. Taking the time to educate your child builds confidence and motivates child to learn.

The sooner you begin with basic skills such as teaching them how to recite and write the alphabet, their first and last names, the more prepared they will be for pre-kindergarten. As your children are promoted from elementary school and move into middle school, class assignments are more difficult for both child and parent.

Homework assignments are more challenging – children have to complete some assignments on the computer, children learn math differently from the way we've learned. Whatever the challenges are, do not give up on children. They need you!

> TIP: Children are a blessing from God, Children are our Future!
> *Dr. Willie J. Kimmons*

PARENTING FOREVER GUIDE INTERACTIVE WORKBOOK WITH ACTIVITIES TO DO WITH YOUR FAMILY by Dr. Willie J. Greer Kimmons & Dr. Gayle S. Ingraham

Topic: Homework

Some of the ways we can teach our children are:

- Believe in your children.
- Get involved with school work.
- Help with homework.
- Encourage school activities.
- Attend PTA Meetings.

Parents are our children's
first teacher

NOTES:

_____

_____

_____

_____

_____

There is an African Proverb that states "it takes a village to raise children". Included in that village are children's schools, parents and teachers who have a great responsibility. In most cases, teachers spend more time with our children than parents do. Teachers are responsible to parent, educate, discipline, support, encourage and motivate children with little or no support or resources.

TIP: Teachers are task masters, motivators, leaders, risk takers, survivors and change agents. In many cases, teachers have made losers and winners. *Dr. Willie J. Kimmons*

PARENTING FOREVER GUIDE INTERACTIVE WORKBOOK WITH ACTIVITIES TO DO WITH YOUR FAMILY by Dr. Willie J. Greer Kimmons & Dr. Gayle S. Ingraham

Topic: Dynamic Teachers

ACTIVITY: In <u>A Parenting Guidebook</u>, read last paragraph on pg. 44 beginning with "I know we can remember when........" After reading this paragraph, discuss the following:

What do you think would happen if your child's teacher disciplined him/her this way today? Please write your answer._____

_____

_____

Parents must take time away from their busy schedules to visit children's schools. Your children can be better supported when teachers know that you care and are concerned about your children's education.

DIRECTIONS: In <u>A Parenting Guidebook</u> pg. 92 "Roles of a Teacher" discuss and complete the following assignment.

List 5 roles of teachers:

  1. _____
  2. _____
  3. _____
  4. _____
  5. _____

DIRECTIONS: In <u>A Parenting Guidebook</u>, pages 97-98, Dr. Kimmons described "good and dynamic" teachers. Let's review, discuss and fill in the blanks below:

- A good teacher has a love of _____ and an intense liking of the _____they teach.
- A good teacher is _____.
- Good teachers get _____ results.
- All teachers can _____.
- Dynamic Teaching is _____ teaching.

Dr. Willie J. Greer Kimmons

PARENTING FOREVER GUIDE INTERACTIVE WORKBOOK WITH ACTIVITIES TO DO WITH YOUR FAMILY by Dr. Willie J. Greer Kimmons & Dr. Gayle S. Ingraham

NOTES:

_____
_____
_____
_____
_____
_____
_____
_____

ROLE PLAY #3

Your daughter, age 13 comes into the living room to grab her book bag before she walks out the door to catch the school bus. You glance at the outfit she has on (short shorts, strapless top – no jacket/sweater, and your high heel shoes)

PARENT: *"you must be losing your mind. I cannot believe you are going to school looking like that. You act just like you do not have any sense at all. Did you look at yourself in the mirror before you came in here? I know my money did not buy that mess you have on. Go to your room right now and take it off. Find something appropriate to wear to school. You better not miss the school bus because you will walk the 5 miles to school. Do you hear me!?"*

NOTES:

_____
_____
_____
_____
_____
_____
_____
_____

PARENTING FOREVER GUIDE INTERACTIVE WORKBOOK WITH ACTIVITIES TO DO WITH YOUR FAMILY by Dr. Willie J. Greer Kimmons & Dr. Gayle S. Ingraham

Help your Children to stay Focused

Time to explore

Research tells us that each child is different. You know your child better than anyone else. Children will go through a series of developmental stages. Each child learns differently so you may need to teach them a little differently. This does not mean that something is wrong with your child. It simply means that you may have to spend a little more time with them.

TIP: All children need parents and positive adults' undivided attention and guidance to help them reach their full potential in school and life.

Dr. Gayle S. Ingraham

Here are a few ways you can HELP your children to stay focused in school:

- If you cannot help your child with homework, get assistance from someone and participate in tutoring sessions with them.
- Take them to the library so that they can get additional educational tools to help them to not fall behind in learning.

Dr. Willie J. Greer Kimmons

PARENTING FOREVER GUIDE INTERACTIVE WORKBOOK WITH ACTIVITIES TO DO WITH YOUR FAMILY by Dr. Willie J. Greer Kimmons & Dr. Gayle S. Ingraham

- Search the internet or watch a You-Tube video with your child that relates to your child's classwork, until you both have an understanding of how to complete the assignment.

- Attend PTA meetings, schedule a special time to meet with the teacher and your child together.

- Ask for help at your child's school.

- Let your child know that you are there for them and support their efforts.

Topic: Help Your Children to Stay Focused

ACTIVITY: Fill in the blanks with these words:
Grades/Language/Self-image/Behavior

Higher _____ Improved _____

Positive _____-_____ Stronger _____ skills

ACTIVITY: In A Parenting Guidebook, read the second paragraph on page 26. Use the following words to fill in the blank for some suggested ways for parents to motivate their child/children to learn:

SUCCESS~STEPS~PROBLEMS~SOLVE~PRAISE
REWARD~MODEL~CURIOSITY

1. Be a _____ of _____
2. _____ and _____ efforts to learn
3. _____real _____
4. Lay out the _____ to _____

1. Make a list of things you enjoy doing with your family and why.

Things I enjoy doing with my children	Why

PARENTING FOREVER GUIDE INTERACTIVE WORKBOOK WITH ACTIVITIES TO DO WITH YOUR FAMILY by Dr. Willie J. Greer Kimmons & Dr. Gayle S. Ingraham

ACTIVITY: Help your children stay focused.

2. Make a list of things I do not like to do with my family and why.

Things I do not enjoy doing with my children	Why?

NOTES:

_____

_____

_____

_____

_____

_____

Topic: Ways to help with school

ACTIVITY: Select one item to practice with a child this week:

1. READ: Take time to read. When you read books magazines and newspapers, you show your child that reading is valuable.
2. WRITE: Write notes to your child. Have your child write grocery lists.
3. SHOW INTEREST: When you show interest in your children's schoolwork, they sense that you care and that you want them to do well.

Take your child
to the library

4. SHOW CURIOSITY: Show your curiosity by asking your child to teach you something she/he learned that day at school. Everyone is a learner – that's the image you want to leave with your child.
5. SHOW PATIENCE: Keep calm and be helpful when things don't go well. Sit down with him/her and say, "Maybe we'll be able to work it out together."

PARENTING FOREVER GUIDE INTERACTIVE WORKBOOK WITH ACTIVITIES TO DO WITH YOUR FAMILY by Dr. Willie J. Greer Kimmons & Dr. Gayle S. Ingraham

Topic: Report Card Discussion

DIRECTIONS: In <u>A Parenting Guidebook</u> pg. 46-48, review Tips for Positive Parenting.

NOTES:

_____

_____

_____

_____

_____

_____

_____

_____

DIRECTIONS: Look at the report card below. How will you respond to your child if this was his/her report card?

Subject/Class	Grade	Comments
Math	D	Grades could improve if homework assignments were turned in.
Reading	B	
Science	A	
Social Studies	F	Missing Assignments
English	D	Distracted in Class

NOTE:

_____

_____

_____

_____

_____

_____

_____

PARENTING FOREVER GUIDE INTERACTIVE WORKBOOK WITH ACTIVITIES TO DO WITH YOUR FAMILY by Dr. Willie J. Greer Kimmons & Dr. Gayle S. Ingraham

> TIP: Take this page out of your workbook and post around the house or in your office or classroom as a reminder!
> **Dr. Willie J. Kimmons**

TRAITS FOR IMPROVING MY CHIILD'S QUALITY OF INSTRUCTION

PTA meeting
time

- Get involved at school.
- Encourage a positive attitude toward school, teachers and schoolwork.
- Ask questions of teachers, administrators and your child about what's going on at school.
- Encourage reading at home.
- Keep a file of your child's work.
- Use praise liberally.

ACTIVITY: Tips for Positive Parenting

> *In* A Parenting Guidebook, *at the bottom of pg. 101- 102 "Teachers, touch a child, touch the future, to reach all, teach all!" Discuss ways that you can model the items listed below and assist your children to ensure their teachers accomplish these…*

- EXPECT RESPECT

  _____

  _____

- REFLECT RESPECT

  _____

  _____

- LEARN TO TEACH DIFFERENCE

  _____

  _____

PARENTING FOREVER GUIDE INTERACTIVE WORKBOOK WITH ACTIVITIES TO DO WITH YOUR FAMILY by Dr. Willie J. Greer Kimmons & Dr. Gayle S. Ingraham

- LET THEM SEE WHAT THEY CAN BE

  _____
  _____

- CONSIDER ALL TO HEAR FROM EACH

  _____
  _____

- ALLOCATE TO ACCOMMODATE

  _____
  _____

- TEST TO GET EACH STUDENT'S BEST

  _____
  _____

- SEPARATE TO EVALUATE

  _____
  _____

- PLACE NO BANDS ON DREAMS AND PLANS

  _____
  _____

- EQUITIZE THEIR WHOLE LIVES

  _____
  _____

NOTES: _____
_____
_____
_____
_____
_____

PARENTING FOREVER GUIDE INTERACTIVE WORKBOOK WITH ACTIVITIES TO DO WITH YOUR FAMILY by Dr. Willie J. Greer Kimmons & Dr. Gayle S. Ingraham

Topic: Tips for Positive Parenting

COMMUNICATION

> DIRECTIONS: In <u>A Parenting Guidebook</u> pages 46-48, review and discuss each section as noted below:

- Be a good role model.
- Never use any kind of physical force on your child.
- Define boundaries (rules) before enforcing them.
- Respond with confident decisiveness when challenged.
- Distinguish between *willful defiance* and *childish irresponsibility.*
- Reassure and teach after the confrontation is over.
- Avoid impossible demands.
- Let love be your guide.

Willful Defiance: *Is a deliberate act of disobedience. It occurs when the child knows what his/her parents expect and is determined to do the opposite.*

Childish Irresponsibility: *results from a child being a child. Being forgetful, having accidents, short attention span, a low tolerance for frustration and the child is immature.*

PARENTING FOREVER GUIDE INTERACTIVE WORKBOOK WITH ACTIVITIES TO DO WITH YOUR FAMILY by Dr. Willie J. Greer Kimmons & Dr. Gayle S. Ingraham

Topic: Tips for Good Communication

DIRECTIONS: In A Parenting Guidebook pages 49-51 under "TIPS FOR GOOD COMMUNICATION", fill in the blanks.

- Always treat children with _____,_____ and _____. (Kindness, Courtesy, Respect)

- _____ actively by repeating your child's feeling with _____ and _____. (Listen, empathy, understanding)

- Avoid _____ with reflective _____. (misunderstandings, listening)

- Cool off before you talk and choose your words _____. (carefully, wisely)

- Remember…if you want to be heard, you first must be _____ and _____. (available, listen)

- Listen _____ and talk _____. (more, less)

- While _____, don't mentally _____ your reply (listening, rehearse)

- Use Plenty of "I" messages

- _____weekly _____. (meetings, Hold)

PARENTING FOREVER GUIDE INTERACTIVE WORKBOOK WITH ACTIVITIES TO DO WITH YOUR FAMILY by Dr. Willie J. Greer Kimmons & Dr. Gayle S. Ingraham

RECOMMENDATIONS FOR THE ACADEMIC SUCCESS OF CHILDREN:

1. Expect the best from _____.
2. Protect all _____.
3. Respect all _____.
4. Believe that all _____can learn.
5. Treat all _____ fairly.
6. Be consistent.
7. Be persistent and _____ will learn.
8. Be enthusiastic about teaching and _____ will be enthusiastic about learning.
9. Reward _____ when they do something right.
10. Reinforce over and over positive behavior around _____.
11. _____imitate adult behavior. Be careful what you do around _____.
12. Be a positive role model for _____,
13. Prepare _____ for learning by being prepared at all times you.
14. Be careful what you say around _____. _____ are very sensitive. If you don't want it repeated, don't' say it around _____.
15. Never openly criticize _____ around other _____.
16. Never tease _____ around other _____. This affects their self-esteem.

PARENTING FOREVER GUIDE INTERACTIVE WORKBOOK WITH ACTIVITIES TO DO WITH YOUR FAMILY by Dr. Willie J. Greer Kimmons & Dr. Gayle S. Ingraham

Topic: Recommendations for the Academic Success of Children

17. Know who you are teaching in your class. It is important to know the _____ background.

18. Your teaching style and teaching techniques should be geared around the caliber of _____ you are teaching.

19. You will never enhance the academic success of _____ if you try to teach them the way you were taught 10, 20, 30 or 40 years ago.

20. Establish a positive relationship with each child's parents or adult figure in the home. Today it takes, teachers, parents and community to train and teach _____.

21. Be patient, compassionate and tolerant with _____, because someone was patient, compassionate and tolerant with you which is why you are here today.

22. Remember that _____ learn at different paces and stages of life.

23. Good teaching techniques and styles are important to enhancing academic success of _____.

24. Remember that there are 3 modalities of learning:
    a. Kinesthetic – Movement and touching
    b. Auditory – hearing
    c. Visual – seeing

25. If _____ can believe it, they can achieve it. _____ who pretend to read will actually learn how to read because they think they can read and their interest in reading is heightened.

26. Test _____ for perfection or mastery, over and over again. This is how _____ learn, by repetition. Repeat material until they learn it and learn it well.

27. The best way to teach _____ how to read is by reading to them, with them, and for them until they like it and can read themselves.

28. We always remember a teacher-good or bad.

29. Practice 21 day concept to learning. If you do something 21 times for 21 days, you will learn to like it, it becomes natural and it becomes a habit. So always practice the 21 day concept with your _____ to enhance their academic success.

PARENTING FOREVER GUIDE INTERACTIVE WORKBOOK WITH ACTIVITIES TO DO WITH YOUR FAMILY by Dr. Willie J. Greer Kimmons & Dr. Gayle S. Ingraham

30. Forging a partnership between parents and teachers to enhance the academic success of _____ will produce these incredible results:

a. Better prepared to enter _____.	a) School
b. Higher _____.	b) Grades
c. Better _____.	c) Behavior
d. Stronger Language _____.	d) Skills
e. Improved _____.	e) Relationships
f. _____ self-image.	f) Positive
g. Pride and _____.	g) Confidence
h. _____.	h) Independence
i. Better _____ to learn.	i) Prepared
j. More likely to become a _____-_____ learner.	j) Life-long

MODULE SIX

HOUSEHOLD MANAGEMENT

Topic: Balancing Finance-Providing for Myself and My Children

GOALS:

- Increase my knowledge of things that my children and I can do together for free.
- Plan and do activities with my children weekly.
- Increase my knowledge of developing a spending plan to have money in savings for the future and emergency.
- Increase my knowledge on household management for myself and my children.

Financial Planning

Whether you are married or single, you do not have to parent alone. Just because you are seeking assistance does not mean that you are not a good parent or you are not coping. Being patient with ourselves, our spouses and children, can reduce stress as we manage our households. Take the time to get your house in order.

NOTE:

PARENTING FOREVER GUIDE INTERACTIVE WORKBOOK WITH ACTIVITIES TO DO WITH YOUR FAMILY by Dr. Willie J. Greer Kimmons & Dr. Gayle S. Ingraham

Balancing Finance

Topic: Providing for myself and my children

What is a budget?

_____

_____

_____

Why do I need a budget?

_____

_____

_____

How do I create a budget?

_____

_____

_____

Who needs a budget?

_____

_____

_____

Household Budget Management:

THINK ABOUT

- ❑ A way to manage the process of paying your bills, purchasing needed items, putting a few dollars in savings
- ❑ How to control your personal finances
- ❑ How much income you will have, how much money you will spend, and how much money will be left over

PARENTING FOREVER GUIDE INTERACTIVE WORKBOOK WITH ACTIVITIES TO DO WITH YOUR FAMILY by Dr. Willie J. Greer Kimmons & Dr. Gayle S. Ingraham

Topic: Providing for my Family

There are several ways to create your family's budget:

THE ENVELOPE SYSTEM

- Have a stack of envelopes labeled one for each bill. Place the amount of cash in each envelope – pay bills in cash/money orders. Great system to use especially if you do not have a checking account.

THE NOTE PAD SYSTEM

- Use the note pad to budget by listing all Income/Expense and using the pad to do all you're budgeting.

SPREAD SHEET

- Using Excel program to develop a spreadsheet that will itemize all expenses/income.

WEB/ONLINE BUDGETS

- Purchasing software, which will track all expenses automatically for you. Some of these systems can be linked to your bank institutions, which will allow you transfer funds from one account to another.
- On line web searches also provide free budget worksheets that are easy to download.

DEBIT CARD AND ATM MACHINE USE

- Use with caution when using your Debit Card and ATM Machines.
- Save your receipts to balance your checkbook at the end of the month.

Words of Caution.....

- If you and your spouse both use ATM machines/Debit cards have a plan for purchases and card use.

PARENTING FOREVER GUIDE INTERACTIVE WORKBOOK WITH ACTIVITIES TO DO WITH YOUR FAMILY by Dr. Willie J. Greer Kimmons & Dr. Gayle S. Ingraham

- It is important that all receipts are given to the person who is responsible for budgeting and paying the bills.
- Each item purchased with debit cards should be deducted from the checkbook immediately.
- Without balancing your checkbook, you set yourself for returned checks and overdraft fees.
- Balancing your checkbook gives you an idea of where you are spending the majority of your money. This will be a great way to keep you on track with your budget.

NOTES:

_____

_____

_____

_____

_____

_____

_____

_____

_____

_____

PARENTING FOREVER GUIDE INTERACTIVE WORKBOOK WITH ACTIVITIES TO DO WITH YOUR FAMILY by Dr. Willie J. Greer Kimmons & Dr. Gayle S. Ingraham

BUDGET WORKSHEET

Directions: Use the list of bills below to practice filling in the budget sheets

LIST OF MONTHLY BILLS TO PAY FOR PRACTICE:

(1)	Rent	$400.00
(2)	Light Bill	$100.00
(3)	Cell Phone Bill	$100.00
(4)	Food	$150.00
(5)	Child Care	$150.00
(6)	Car Insurance	$150.00
(7)	Car Payment	$300.00
(8)	Cable	$200.00
(9)	Credit Cards	$100.00
(10)	Student Loan	$100.00

INCOME:

Monthly Income	$1500.00
Other Income	$ 240.00

NOTES:

_____

_____

_____

_____

_____

_____

_____

_____

_____

_____

PARENTING FOREVER GUIDE INTERACTIVE WORKBOOK WITH ACTIVITIES TO DO WITH YOUR FAMILY by Dr. Willie J. Greer Kimmons & Dr. Gayle S. Ingraham

Topic: Our Family Budget

Month of: _____ Year: _____

Category	Budget Amount	Actual Amount	Difference
INCOME			
Income Total			
EXPENSES			
EXPENSES SUB-TOTAL			
NET INCOME (Income – Expenses)			

PARENTING FOREVER GUIDE INTERACTIVE WORKBOOK WITH ACTIVITIES TO DO WITH YOUR FAMILY by Dr. Willie J. Greer Kimmons & Dr. Gayle S. Ingraham

Month of: _____

CATEGORY	Budget Amount	Actual Amount	Difference
INCOME			
Income			
Income			
Other Income			
Other Income			
Income Total			
EXPENSES			
Charitable Contributions			
Rent/Mortgage			
Electric Bill			
Home Phone			
Cell Phone			
Cable TV			
Car Payment			
Bus Passes			
Car Insurance			
Car Repairs			
Emergency Savings			
Long Term Savings			
School Loan			
Child Care			
Credit Cards			
EXPENSES SUB-TOTAL			
NET INCOME (Income – Expenses)			

PARENTING FOREVER GUIDE INTERACTIVE WORKBOOK WITH ACTIVITIES TO DO WITH YOUR FAMILY by Dr. Willie J. Greer Kimmons & Dr. Gayle S. Ingraham

Topic: How to Balance Your Checkbook

Where to begin:

- You need a copy of your bank account statement for the previous month.
- Your checkbook register or spreadsheet where you recorded your purchases and withdrawals.
- Calculator or adding machine

Step 1:

- In your checkbook, locate each deposit listed by the bank on the statement. Check them off in your checkbook where the deposit is listed.

Step 2:

- Put an (X) next to the deposits that are not listed on your bank statement next to all of the deposits that you have that do not appear on the bank's statement. These deposits are considered outstanding and will show up on the next month statement.

Step 3:

- Repeat the process above with all of the debit transactions.

Step 4:

- Repeat the process above with all of the checks written
- Do not forget to list all services charges as well as ATM charges and deduct or add accordingly.

Step 5:

- Find the bank's ending balance and write this on a separate piece of paper.
- To the bank ending balance, add all of the outstanding deposits from your checkbook (the deposits with "X" next to them. This total reflects all of the deposits made by you.

PARENTING FOREVER GUIDE INTERACTIVE WORKBOOK WITH ACTIVITIES TO DO WITH YOUR FAMILY by Dr. Willie J. Greer Kimmons & Dr. Gayle S. Ingraham

Step 6:

- Next, deduct all of the outstanding debits and checks from steps #3 and #4 above.
- The balance should equal the balance you have in your checkbook.

TIP: If you have never balanced your checkbook, you may have to look at the previous month's bank statement to determine which checks that are still outstanding. **Dr. Gayle Ingraham**

- Avoid payday cash/loan services.
- Schedule time to meet with your bank representative about savings, checking and credit repairs.

MODULE SEVEN

FINDING SUPPORT AND COMMUNITY RESOURCES

Topic: Finding Support And Community Resources For My Family

GOALS:

Learn about resources in
your community

- Explore at least 10 things you and your child can do for free.
- Learn about a support group that my family and I can attend.
- Learn about community resources and how to access them.

For this module, we will share a few ideas or from organizations that provide additional support and community resources to families. We will also discuss some of the resources that you are familiar with and create a list to share.

Today's technology has made it much easier for family to find needed support. However, if you are not computer savvy you can seek the assistance through your local church or community organizations.

PARENTING FOREVER GUIDE INTERACTIVE WORKBOOK WITH ACTIVITIES TO DO WITH YOUR FAMILY by Dr. Willie J. Greer Kimmons & Dr. Gayle S. Ingraham

Emotional Support

> TIPS: There are numerous kinds of community volunteer programs from mentoring, tutoring, after school, child care, big brothers, big sisters, PTA's PTO's, YMCA, to various clubs. The key things they all have in common are building better schools, children and communities. ***Dr. Willie J. Kimmons***

"We all can use support from time to time."

Emotional Support, Practical Support, Social Support

Support from others come in three ways:

Siblings need support too!

(1) ***E*** _____
    S _____, that helps us cope better with all the issues with parenting, especially when we receive the support from someone with experience.

(2) ***P***_____ ***S***_____ to help us better balance workload, finances.

(3) ***S***_____ ***S***_____ which provides parents an opportunity to spend time with other adults and/or participate in social events that provide respite from children.

PARENTING FOREVER GUIDE INTERACTIVE WORKBOOK WITH ACTIVITIES TO DO WITH YOUR FAMILY by Dr. Willie J. Greer Kimmons & Dr. Gayle S. Ingraham

LAYAWAY:

List department stores that have layaway services:

_____

_____

_____

_____

BACK TO SCHOOL FAIRS

Make a list of community organizations that provide back to school events in your area:

_____

_____

_____

_____

BOGO Sales:

Discuss the value of Buy One Get One items. Share ideas within your group of where to get the best deals:

_____

_____

_____

_____

FOOD ITEMS:

List food banks in your area:

_____

_____

_____

_____

PARENTING FOREVER GUIDE INTERACTIVE WORKBOOK WITH ACTIVITIES TO DO WITH YOUR FAMILY by Dr. Willie J. Greer Kimmons & Dr. Gayle S. Ingraham

TIP: If you spend time on the local School District's Website, you may find more information about free items to students who participate in free and/or reduced lunch programs.
Dr. Gayle S. Ingraham

List possible resources that your children's school can provide:

_____

_____

_____

_____

_____

_____

_____

_____

_____

_____

TIP: Take your Driver's License or ID card, social security card and a utility bill with your name and address on it. You may also be required to take some form of ID for everyone living in the house with you. **Dr. Gayle Ingraham**

PARENTING FOREVER GUIDE INTERACTIVE WORKBOOK WITH ACTIVITIES TO DO WITH YOUR FAMILY by Dr. Willie J. Greer Kimmons & Dr. Gayle S. Ingraham

COMMUNITY RESOURCE SHEET

Directions: Use the form below to list all of the community resources you use in your area. Once your list is completed share it with the others in your group.

ORGANIZATION'S NAME	SERVICES PROVIDED	WEBSITE/CONTACT INFORMATION

SUMMARY

Hopefully, this Parenting Forever Workbook will serve as some assistance to all of us who have interest in helping to rear and provide guidance for children, especially parents. As long as we have human beings, we will always have our children.

The youth diversion program is to remind parents, grandparents and significant adults in the home that they will be held accountable for their children's actions. Through the 3 Saturdays required training program, hopefully it will reassure parents that raising children is their responsibility. The workshop training will provide the necessary tools during the required 3 Saturdays for parents. The parents will be required to do a better job of providing some pride, dignity, value, respect for others and self-respect for the child. The 7 modules will be interactive with a great deal of hands on training as well as role modeling activities.

Finally, the youth diversion program for youths and parents is to ultimately reduce crime and give the parents and youths an alternative plan to eliminate jail time. Once the youth is in the prison system, the options are less and we would have lost another child. This diversion program is different than other programs that's geared towards the juvenile. Our Parenting Forever Workbook 3 Saturdays required training is to assist parents, grandparents and significant adults in the home to take the responsibility for their children actions. This is why having a partnership through a collaborative effort with the department of Juvenile Justice that's approved by the State Attorney's Office is necessary for the program to be successful. Parent by parent, youth by youth, community by community, all concerned citizens should have a moral, personal and professional obligation to ensure that no child is left behind.

The 3 Saturdays required training workshop for parents will be supplemented with a copy of the Parenting Guidebook authored by Dr. Willie J. Greer-Kimmons as part of the training.

BIBLIOGRAPHY

Black, T., Straight Talk About American Education, Harcourt Brace Jovanovich, New York, 1982.

Buskin, Martin, Parent Power, Walker and Company, New York, 1975.

Clark, Faye & Frank 1998. They're All Our Children, and their Crusade to Educate the Children:

Educate the Children Foundation, New York, New York.

Comer, James P. and Poussaint, Alvin F. (1976). Black Child Care. New York, New York. Pocket Books, Simon and Schuster, Inc.

Crosby, Margaree S. 30 December 2000. Speech at the National Childcare Institute Conference, "The important Role Parental Involvement Plays in Rearing Children of Color," Jacksonville, Florida.

Dobson, James, (1987). Dare to Discipline. Tyndale House Publishers, Wheaton, Il.

Dreikurs, Rudolf, and Grey, Loren (1970). A Parent's Guide to Child Discipline: A Modern System For Raising Modern Children. New York, New York: Hawthorn Books, Inc.

Fege, Arnold F. (2000). From Fun Raising to Hell Raising: New Roles for Parents Educational Leadership, v.57 no.7 (April 2000). 1-43. Retrieved from FirstSearch database on May 13, 2003 http://www.firstsearch@ocla.org

Hiemstra, R., The Educative Community, Linking the Community School, and Family, Professional Educators Publication, Inc., Lincoln, Nebraska, 1972.

Ingraham, Gayle S., A Qualitative Study of Why Grandparent Caregivers Attend Kinship Services Network Pinellas Support Groups. A Doctoral Dissertation. Submitted to the Faculty of Argosy University, Tampa Campus, College of Education. In Partial

Fulfillment of The Requirements of the Degree of Doctor of Education. (March, 2013).

Ingraham, Gayle S. "Ingraham Parenting Stages". Workshop Presentation at the 2015 Youth Annual Conference Hillsborough Community College – Trinkle Center - Plant City Campus (July 2015).

Kimmons, Willie J. Greer, The Role of School/Community in Rearing Children, A Parenting Guidebook, AuthorHouse, Bloomington, Indiana, 2012.

Langston, Teresa (1993). Parenting Without Pressure. A Parent's Guide. NAV Press, Colorado Springs CO

O'Connor, Grace. (1966) Helping Your Children: A Basic Guide for Parents. Austin, Texas: Steck-Vaughn Company.

Paige, Rod, (April 8, 2002). Schools Can't Improve Without Help of Parents. Retrieved from the

Worldwide Web, USA Today, 7 June 2002. "httpww.usatoday.com"

ABOUT THE AUTHOR

Dr. *Willie J. Greer Kimmons*

Dr. Kimmons is one of America's leading authorities on higher education, leadership. Parental involvement and health related issues. He is a nationally recognized consultant, speaker, seminar leader and author of 7 books. He spent his entire career understanding the nature of today's students, teachers and parents. He also serves as a national spokesperson on health issues. Dr. Kimmons holds a Bachelor of Science Degree in Health Education and Psychology; a Master of Science Degree in Curriculum and Instruction; and a Doctorate Degree in Educational Administration & Supervision in Higher Education. He has spent the last 40 years in a range of professions from public school teacher, military officer, college dean and vice president to president and chancellor in two and four year colleges and universities. Dr. Kimmons' outstanding performances support his life's ambition to expand his commitment and dedication to the learner. Dr. Kimmons' Parenting Guidebook's Foreword was written by his Godmother, The late Great Honorable Shirley Chisholm, First African American female to be elected in 1968 to the U.S. Congress and the first female to run for the office of the President of the United States in 1972.

ABOUT THE CO-AUTHOR

Dr. Gaye S. Ingraham

Dr. Gayle Ingraham is a consultant for Not-For-Profit Organizations. She has been instrumental in the development of training and workshop curriculum for a variety of organizations.

Dr. Ingraham holds a Bachelor of Science Degree in Criminal Justice and Business Management; a Master Degree in Education and a Doctorate Degree in Educational Leadership.

Dr. Ingraham has spent the past 20 years in a range of professions that include Project Development Evaluator, Program Management, Professional Development Consultant, Counseling, Social Work, Behavioral Specialist, Workshop Presenter and Trainer.

Printed in the United States
by Baker & Taylor Publisher Services